SCARBOROUGH
HISTORY TOUR

Dedicated to the memory of my late wife, Hilary,
who loved seeing her name in print

First published 2020

Amberley Publishing
The Hill, Stroud,
Gloucestershire, GL5 4EP
www.amberley-books.com

Copyright © Mike Hitches, 2020
Map contains Ordnance Survey data
© Crown copyright and database
right [2020]

The right of Mike Hitches to be
identified as the Author of this work
has been asserted in accordance with
the Copyrights, Designs and Patents
Act 1988.

ISBN 978 1 3981 0062 6 (print)
ISBN 978 1 3981 0063 3 (ebook)

British Library Cataloguing in
Publication Data.
A catalogue record for this book is
available from the British Library.

Origination by Amberley Publishing.
Printed in Great Britain.

INTRODUCTION

Scarborough started as a resort when a spring was discovered by local lady Elizabeth Farrow coming out of South Bay cliff in 1602. She claimed that health-giving benefits were derived from the water there. At that period, spring water spas were becoming popular as people wanted to experience these health-giving properties. The water at Scarborough brought many new people as it supposedly helped to cure constipation. With the popularity of the spring here, the town began to prosper and grow. Such was the popularity of Scarborough that in 1698 a new sea wall was built and a cistern was established for the spa waters. A landslide in the early eighteenth century buried the spring and a new, much grander spa building was established.

Scarborough expanded even further when Victorians believed that sea bathing and sea air was good for them. This, at first, brought many wealthy people to the town to benefit from the sea and air, as well as escaping from the overcrowded, dirty and smoky towns in the West Riding of Yorkshire. To accommodate this influx of new people, many new establishments were built. The arrival of the railway into Scarborough in around 1845 allowed more visitors to the town and the advent of cheap excursion tickets allowed working-class people to share the pleasures of the resort and the town expanded further.

Scarborough's history, however, goes back much further. The first record of the place was as early as AD 370 when the Romans established a signalling station on the headland, which, today, separates the north shore and south shore. The south shore is the most popular, while the north shore is much quieter. The signal station was set up as an early warning to protect the area from attack by the Anglo-Saxons. After the Romans left, the Anglo-Saxons moved in from around AD 410, followed by the Vikings around AD 966. In the same year as the famous Battle of Hastings in 1066, the Norwegians burned down the town.

The headland was ideal as a fortress and a castle was built on the site by the Earl of Albermarle in 1130. It was eventually captured by Henry II and it became a royal castle. In the years that followed, the castle was subject to many attacks and sieges.

In 1235, Henry III gave the town a royal charter to hold an annual fair, which is still remembered and made famous by Simon and Garfunkel's version of the song 'Scarborough Fair'.

By the early seventeenth century, Scarborough – the name being derived from Norseman Thorsgill who had a cleft lip and was given the nickname 'Scarthi' and the hill where the castle now stands being named 'Burg' in Norse, which was corrupted to the modern name – had fallen into decline and was only saved by the discovery of the spring. The town, by this time, was centred on Eastborough, Friargate, Tollergate and Longwestgate and was centred on the fishing trade. It was also, by 1785, involved in shipbuilding and around fifteen ships were launched each year. A floating dock was also built to allow ships to come in for repair.

The town has grown much over the last centuries and some of the old landmarks are still around today, along with newer structures that show how Scarborough has evolved.

KEY

1. Scarborough Railway Station
2. Westborough
3. St Thomas Street
4. St Nicholas Street
5. The Grand Hotel
6. Cliff Bridge
7. The Esplanade
8. The Crown Spa Hotel
9. Church Parade
10. The Italian Garden
11. The Royal
12. Scarborough Spa Complex
13. South Bay Beach
14. Foreshore Road
15. The Harbour
16. The Lighthouse
17. Old Town
18. The Castle
19. Marine Drive
20. Scarborough Pier
21. North Bay Beach
22. Clarence Gardens
23. Corner Café
24. The Open Air Theatre
25. Peasholm Park
26. The Lake
27. Scarborough Cricket Ground
28. North Marine Drive

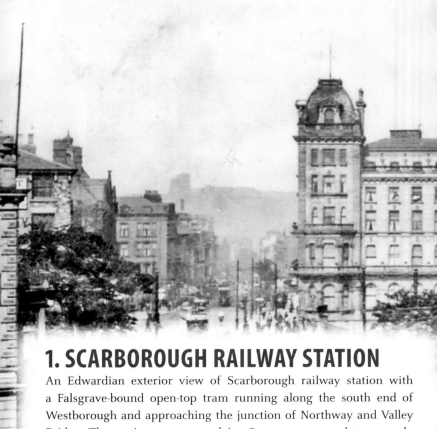

1. SCARBOROUGH RAILWAY STATION

An Edwardian exterior view of Scarborough railway station with a Falsgrave-bound open-top tram running along the south end of Westborough and approaching the junction of Northway and Valley Bridge. The station was opened in 1845 to accommodate a newly inaugurated train service from York, which, in turn, connected the town with cities in the West Riding and allowed the resort to boom as tourism expanded due to the railway. The clock on the tower was built by Potts of Leeds at a cost of £110, and remains a prominent landmark today.

Interior of Scarborough Station

Interior of the station in the early twentieth century. The station was designed by the York & North Midland Railway architect George Andrews and contained all of the facilities expected by the nineteenth-century traveller. The overall roof, however, was only completed a few years after opening.

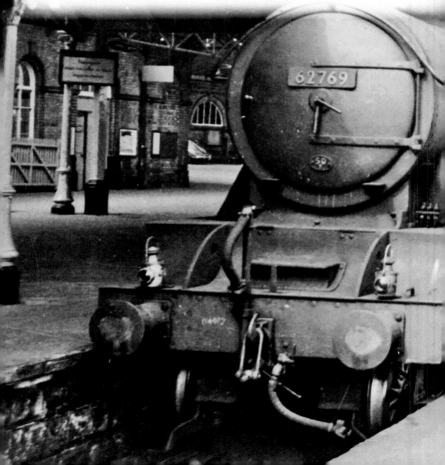

Ex-LNER Class D49 4-4-0 steam locomotive No. 62735 *Westmorland* waits to depart from Scarborough station with a train for York. Although main-line steam traction ended in the 1960s, special steam excursions arrive from York during the summer months. The inset view shows ex-LMS 'Princess Royal' pacific No. 6201 *Princess Elizabeth* at the station in 2007.

Modern traction, in the form of diesel multiple units, changed the face of the station in this 1965 view.

A passenger train arrives at Scarborough in North Eastern Railway days with 4-4-0 locomotive No. 1629, built in 1893, at its head.

A 1930s view of Scarborough station, with the Scarborough Flyer train departing for York. Nearest is a steam railmotor train, favoured by the LNER as they were relatively cheap to run on local branch lines, about to depart for Whitby.

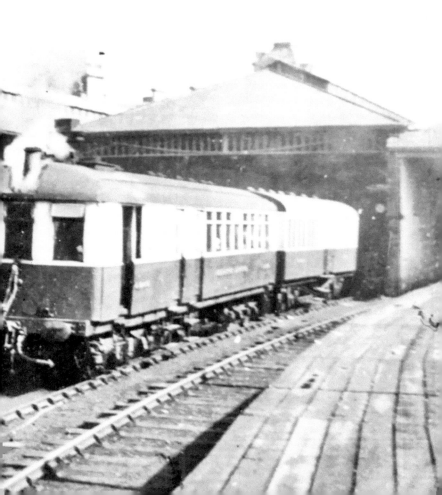

SCARBOROUGH. LNER.

Another D49 4-4-0 No. 62735 Westmorland awaits its turn of duty at Scarborough station on the same day.

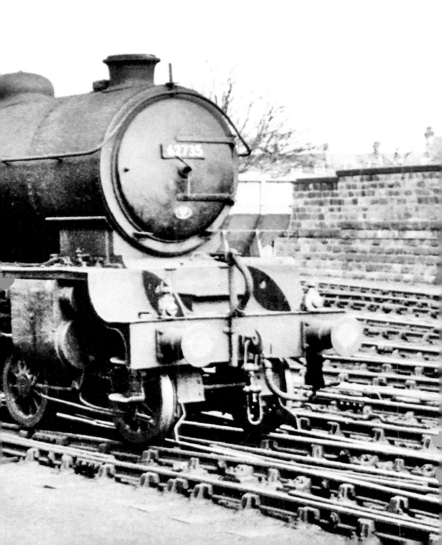

Ex-LNER A8 Class 4-6-2 tank engine No. 69886 is seen passing Falsgrave signalbox with an empty stock train on 29 July 1955. In view is the signal gantry, signal box and wooden platform, which served excursion trains at Scarborough. Behind the signal box and out of view is the tunnel that formed the start of the line to Whitby. In 2010, the signal box had fallen out of use, but it is a listed building and remains in situ. The track here has been rationalised and the platform is now out of use. The signal gantry would be removed in a few months' time. A new building, constructed in connection with resignalling at the station, can be seen behind the platform and is the reason why the signal gantry is to disappear. The new building hides the now blocked up tunnel of the Whitby branch, which actually closed in 1963, and was one of the reasons why traffic declined at Scarborough.

To provide locomotives for services out of Scarborough, the railway companies provided a loco shed here, seen as it was in the 1930s when under LNER ownership. In view are an A8 4-6-2T and an LNER 816 4-6-0. Below is the loco shed on 2 June 1963, just after it was closed. In the background is the gasworks at Seamer Road, which itself has disappeared with the arrival of natural gas. Between the shed and the gasworks can be seen the gantry for the main line into Scarborough station.

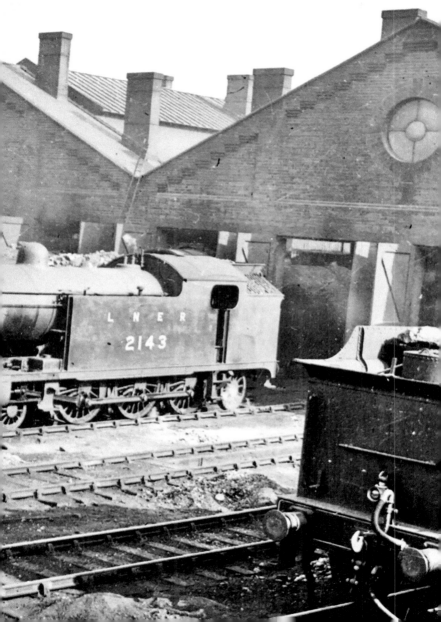

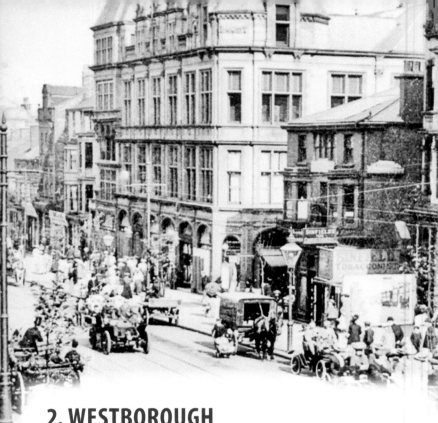

2. WESTBOROUGH

The main shopping street is at Westborough, seen here in the Edwardian period. Horse-drawn charabancs are heading in the direction of the railway station carrying passengers through the town. Virtually all transport at this time was horse drawn. The shops here are advertising some products that are still with us today, such as Cadbury's chocolate. Just behind the first charabanc is a tobacconist shop, a rare sight today. The modern Westborough is now pedestrianised and only delivery vehicles can use the road. Often, in the summer, a street market occupies the pedestrian street.

3. ST THOMAS STREET

St Thomas Street links Westborough with North Marine Road and this Edwardian view shows Boots the Chemist on the corner with its fine window display. Boots still has a presence in the town and its location is opposite the Brunswick Centre on Westborough.

4. ST NICHOLAS STREET

A view of South Bay from St Nicholas Street with Scarborough Castle in the background. Just below, on the left, is the shed for the South Cliff Railway, which brings passengers up the steep incline at this point.

5. THE GRAND HOTEL

A major feature of the South Bay is the Grand Hotel, which opened in 1867. This multistorey building once had 365 rooms on seven floors and occupies the site of No. 2 The Cliff where Anne Brontë stayed during the summer months. She contracted tuberculosis and died while staying at the house. Her body was buried in the town.

6. CLIFF BRIDGE

Cliff Bridge was opened in 1827 and links the Grand Hotel with the Esplanade and is also a connection with the spa complex. It is a popular spot with visitors as it provides views of both the Esplanade and South Bay with its beach.

BRIDGE, *Scarborough.*

7. THE ESPLANADE

The Esplanade during the Edwardian period. Ladies can be seen strolling along the footpath in the fashions of the day, which must have been heavy and uncomfortable in the summer. They carried parasols to shade them from the sunshine and to prevent 'tanning', which was considered 'common' in those days. Gentlemen, seated on the bench, wore suits with either a peaked cap or straw boater hats during the summer. In the centre background is the Crown Hotel, flanked by terraces of apartments and smaller hotels. The Crown Hotel was served by a cliff railway, the first of its kind in England when opened in 1875, linking the hotel to the spa complex and saving visitors a climb of 224 steps.

8. THE CROWN SPA HOTEL

Still a high-class hotel, the Crown Spa Hotel added the 'Spa' to its original name in recent years and now holds conferences during the winter months and is busy with visitors during the summer.

SCARBOROUGH. CHURCH PARADE

9. CHURCH PARADE

The Esplanade, Crown Hotel and terraces on a busy Edwardian summer Sunday as visitors and locals alike promenade for Church Parade. The Grand Hotel, South Bay beach and its attractions, along with the Old Town, are in the far background.

10. THE ITALIAN GARDEN

Just below the Esplanade and heading towards the rocky shore lies the Italian Garden, established in the early years of the twentieth century and still in existence today. Just further along the coast once lay the Holbeck Hotel, which gained national fame when it collapsed into the sea due to coastal erosion in 1995. Its demise was reported by both the BBC and ITV. Coastal erosion continues to be a problem here and bungalows between Scarborough and Cayton Bay are under threat of disappearing into the sea.

11. THE ROYAL

At the junction of the Esplanade and Holbeck Road is the house that found fame as the location for the ITV series *The Royal*, about life in a 1950s hospital. The series was a spin-off from another series filmed near Whitby, *Heartbeat*, and both programmes were often interlinked. Opposite The Royal was the clock tower, still in situ, which was often seen in the series.

12. SCARBOROUGH SPA COMPLEX

The original Scarborough Spa complex was built in the 1850s to a design by Joseph Paxton. This original building did not survive due to a fire in 1876, the whole area being totally rebuilt afterwards. The new complex lasted for nearly a century until substantial refurbishment took place. The spa complex held events, often catering for Christmas parties. In earlier days, the Palm Court Orchestra would play here and the modern Spa Orchestra still entertains during the summer season.

PA, SCARBORO

13. SOUTH BAY BEACH

A 1950s view of the South Bay beach at Scarborough, which is seen from the pathway that leads from the Esplanade. The promenade entrance to the Grand Hotel is visible on the left, which is long gone today. The sands are quite busy but there are very few motor vehicles running along Foreshore Road at this time – so different from today.

SOUTH BAY AND SANDS, SCA

Sea Bathing Infirmary. Scarborough

14. FORESHORE ROAD

The Sea Bathing Infirmary is the main feature among the shops in this 1920s view. The benefits of the sea in aiding health is still apparent at this time. Although the building still exists, its use as an infirmary has long gone and it is now a fancy goods shop on the ground floor while the upper floors were offered for rent.

15. THE HARBOUR

The harbour was once the commercial and industrial centre of Scarborough. The fishing boats, known as 'cobles' on the east coast, are seen at the quay. In the late nineteenth century, women were at the harbour gutting fish before going for sale. Visitors can be seen watching proceedings while, in the background, the rather ornate tollbooth can be seen at the entrance to the North Bay. Nowadays, the area is taken up by a fairground, but the tollbooth still stands, though it is out of use.

With the Grand Hotel in the background, the paddle steamer *Bilsdale* is approaching Scarborough Harbour during the summer of 1927. The *Bilsdale's* captain, C. W. Duncan, is inset top left. Inset top right passing through Scarborough on her final voyage, is *Cunarder Mauretania* on 2 July 1935. Before the First World War, the liner used

P.S. BILSDALE

to call at Fishguard before going on to Liverpool, as passengers could reach London quicker by rail from there instead of sailing through to Liverpool and thence to the capital. Her sister ship, the *Lusitania*, was sunk by a German U-boat off the Old Head of Kinsale, to the west of Ireland, in 1915, which did much to bring the USA into the war.

Scarborough . 1927.

16. THE LIGHTHOUSE

This 1895 view shows the lighthouse and fish quay with boats arriving from the North Sea with their fish. The lighthouse suffered some damage when the town was shelled by a German battleship in 1914 after the outbreak of the First World War. The event was used as a way of recruiting soldiers for the army, using the slogan 'Remember Scarborough'.

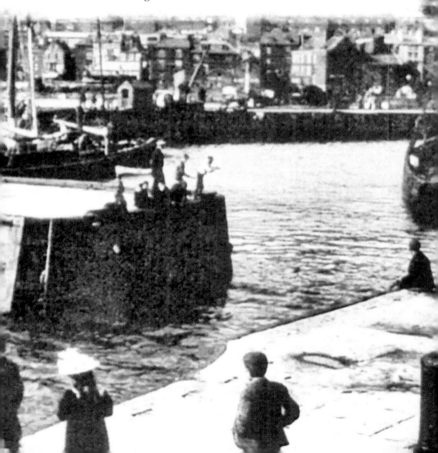

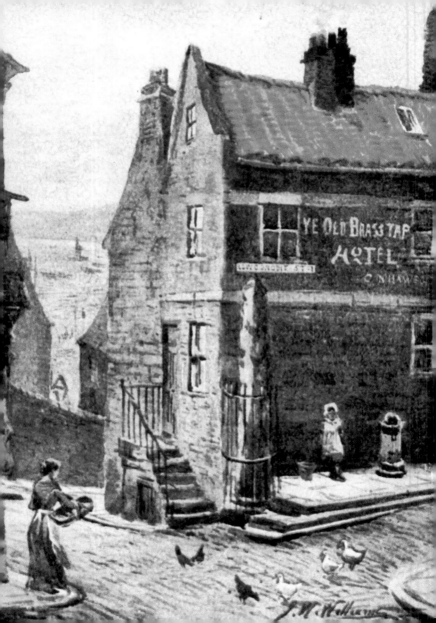

17. OLD TOWN

Three eighteenth-century views of Old Town, nestled up on high ground close to the castle, which was centred round St Mary's Church. The church is seen looking up at the steps on what is now Church Steps Street. The other views show Old Butter Cross with Ye Old Tap Hotel in view on Low Conduit Street. The other view shows a steep hill with St Mary's Church in the background. These streets no longer exist but were in the area now filled by Castle Gardens and Castle Terrace. The recent television show *Scarborough* was mostly filmed in the modern 'Old Town'.

18. THE CASTLE

The castle ruins are seen here in this pre-Second World War view with North Bay in the background. A castle has existed in the town since 1136 when William le Gros obtained permission from King Stephen for its construction. It was captured by Henry II and, by 1168, it became a royal fortress. Over the years since then the castle has been besieged twice during the English Civil War and it was attacked by German ships when they shelled the town in 1914, which damaged the curtain wall.

NORTH BAY · FROM
CASTLE · SCARBOROUGH

19. MARINE DRIVE

An Edwardian view of Marine Drive on a blustery day. Visitors look cold and wet as they watch yachts battling with the rough North Sea. Marine Drive is the entrance to North Bay and it goes round the headland on which the ruins of the castle stand.

20. SCARBOROUGH PIER

A pier at Scarborough was built on the North Bay by the famous pier builder Eugenius Birch and completed in 1869 at a cost of £16,000. Unfortunately, the pier was built in the wrong place because this part of the coast suffered badly from stormy weather. Such an event took place on 8 January 1905 and brought about its collapse. It was never replaced.

21. NORTH BAY BEACH

Bathing machines are in profusion in this 1891 view of the beach at North Bay, the men and women dressed in the Victorian fashions of the day. Bathing machines were introduced to the seaside to protect the modesty of the ladies at this time, when females were objects of mystery and ladies' legs were not to be seen. Bikinis, swimsuits and swimming trunks were not appropriate dress at that time. It has been said that Scarborough was the first seaside resort to introduce bathing machines. In the background is the end of the pier with its theatre in view. Here Pierrot shows were held, a favourite entertainment of Victorians. Modern chalets (inset overleaf) have long replaced bathing machines.

22. CLARENCE GARDENS

Victorian holidaymakers enjoyed peace and quiet, along with floral displays, which go hand in hand with the pursuit of heathy fresh air away from the smoky industrial towns of the West Riding from which many of these Victorians made their fortunes. Clarence Gardens on North Bay provided such facilities and can be seen here in 1897. The entrance to the pier opposite was just left of the flagpole. On top of the cliff in the background are the hotels and apartments that provided accommodation in those days.

14525. SCARBOROUGH. NORTH BAY. CORNER CA

23. CORNER CAFÉ

A 1930s view of the Corner Café, which provided refreshments for holidaymakers on North Bay. In the 1990s plans were drawn up to replace the café with a more modern structure leading up to Peasholm Park and providing a modern complex of flats for sale, which gives an unobstructed view of the bay and castle. A café and supermarket are situated on the ground floor. The complex is seen opposite in 2011.

24. THE OPEN AIR THEATRE

A landscaped park area connects North Bay with the Open Air Theatre. Constructed by Scarborough Borough Council, the theatre was opened in 2010 to replace one that had been built on Northstead Manor Gardens in 1932 and closed in 1986. The inset shows the old theatre during a production of *Hiawatha* in the 1930s.The modern theatre presents concerts by well-known artists during the summer months.

PHOTO BY H.O.T. SCARBORO'   HIAWATHA   OPEN AIR THEATRE, SCARBOROUGH   1736

25. PEASHOLM PARK

A view of Peasholm Park in the early twentieth century, depicting the glen with its lily pond. The park lies at the end of Royal Albert Drive, which also contains a miniature railway and the Open Air Theatre.

26. THE LAKE

Peasholm Park Lake has Japanese features, complete with lanterns. The lake is also used in the summer to give displays of sea battles using model ships (opposite), which is popular with visitors.

MODEL WARSHIP IN "THE BATTLE OF THE

PLATE" PEASHOLM LAKE SCARBOROUGH

27. SCARBOROUGH CRICKET GROUND

The cricket ground on North Marine Drive has been in the town since 1878 and is used by Yorkshire County Cricket Club for county matches and one-day games, particularly during Scarborough Festival. The North Marine Drive entrance to the cricket ground is seen here in 2011. Football is also played in the town. Scarborough Football Club was established in 1879 and even played in League One until misfortune befell it when the club ran up debts of £2.5 million and was wound up in 2007. The club was resurrected in the same year as Scarborough Athletic and started playing in the Northern Counties League as it started the long climb back.

28. NORTH MARINE DRIVE

North Marine Drive links North Bay with South Bay via St Thomas Street. In the early years of the twentieth century, a military parade is passing along North Marine Drive. Its hotels and apartments are in the background.

ABOUT THE AUTHOR

A native of Birmingham, Mike is a retired staff nurse living in the North Yorkshire seaside resort of Filey, which lies equidistant between Scarborough and Bridlington. He has also lived in North Wales and Manchester.

Mike obtained a social sciences degree from Bangor University in the 1980s and went on to lecture in sociology at night classes before starting a writing career. He studied for his nursing diploma in the 1990s and went on to specialise in cardiology.

He is widowed and has two sons and a granddaughter who is very precious to him because she is the first girl in his family for three generations.

Mike sometimes gives talks on various local topics and volunteers at a local charity shop and local library.